Undeniable Breakthrough

Transform Your Life and Defeat Everything That's Blocking Your Blessings

Spiritual Guide and Life Journal

RAINIE HOWARD

Rainie Howard Enterprises LLC. Publishing Agency
Saint Louis, MO 63108

Scripture quotations are taken from the Holy Bible.

For information about special discounts for bulk purchases or bringing the author to your live event, please contact Rainie Howard Enterprises Sales

at 314-827-5216 or Contact@RainieHoward.com
Manufactured in the United State of America

ISBN-13: 978-1537515601

ISBN-10: 1537515608

Also by Rainie Howard:

ADDICTED TO PAIN

WHEN GOD SENT MY HUSBAND

CONTENTS

ACKNOWLEDGMENTS

I want to thank my wonderful and amazing husband, Patrick Howard. I love you so much. Special thanks to my children, Patrick "Bj" and Aniyah Howard.

I love you with all my heart.

INTRODUCTION

We've all been there, that place where your wants become passionate desires that feel like extreme needs. We pray for what we want, cry for it, meditate on it and beg for it, but despite all the yearning and pleading, we're left empty-handed. It's almost torturous to desire something so badly but never receive it. It's in that moment of desperation that your prayer becomes, "Lord bless me with an undeniable breakthrough."

You may have been seeking a breakthrough in your love life, family, finances or even in your health. Maybe for you it's all the above. You're tired of struggling and lacking. You're tired of living in "just-enough land," and you want to live in the land of plenty. You desire abundance in your life, and you want to know why you lack what you see others receive. To see others live lives filled with breakthrough blessings is only a reminder of what you don't have.

You may feel as if you've done the work and there's nothing left for you to do, or maybe you feel like you must be missing something, like there's something you're supposed to do that you aren't aware of. In this book, you will learn the strategy for transforming your life and defeating everything that's blocking you from receiving an undeniable breakthrough. You will learn how to:

- Think differently
- Create life-changing habits that bring results
- Endure every challenge and struggle that comes your way

By the end of this guide and journal, you will be prepared to experience an undeniable breakthrough in your life. This journal was produced to be completed in the "Undeniable Breakthrough Bundle," which includes several videos and audio downloads that are available to purchase at www.RealLoveExist.com. Lets get your breakthrough!

LIFE MESSAGE 1

THE SHOCKING TRUTH

"Every breakthrough experienced in my life was the result of me breaking down and surrendering it all to God."

–Rainie Howard

From the title of this first chapter, you are probably already wondering what the shocking truth is, and I'm going to get to that, but first let's understand what makes something shocking. Webster's defines shocking as "very surprising and upsetting or causing a sudden feeling of horror or disgust."

Now that you know that what you're about to find out may be surprising or upsetting, let's get to the truth by understanding the deceiving lie. We live in a culture that pities and despises those who are jobless, disabled and poor. At the same time, our culture promotes self-made-millionaires, self-proclaimed motivational speakers, bestselling authors, celebrities and entrepreneurs. Sometimes it can be discouraging to individuals who aren't rich and famous. Often, we are encouraged to "fake it until you make it."

This "fake it until you make it" mindset can be detrimental to an individual's authenticity and their truth and damaging to society. It has created a society of countless get-rich-quick schemes, global economic devastations and millions of fraudulent people planting seeds of deception in families, communities, governments, entertainments and cultures.

This mindset encourages the belief that you should be able to have whatever you want almost as soon as you want it. But the shocking truth is that you cannot have whatever you want instantly. Your breakthrough will not happen overnight. You will not get it through a get-rich-quick scam. True love doesn't come at first sight. If you're feeling horrified and upset, it's because you've been believing a lie. You ate the lie our society is feeding us all.

Here's the truth about breakthroughs. Breakthroughs often come out of brokenness, not out of not bragging or making people believe you are someone you're not. The truth is that it takes an overwhelming breakdown in order to experience an undeniable breakthrough.

"Wealth from get-rich-quick schemes quickly disappears; wealth from hard work grows over time." (Proverbs 13:11)

The truth is that you will be blessed when you are faithful enough to consistently do what God has called you to do. Your breakthrough will manifest after you've completed your tests and trials while trusting God and seeking Him daily. Proverbs 22:29 says, "Do you see a man diligent in his work? He shall stand before kings." This means that no matter where you are currently in your life, if you are faithful and diligent in following God's plan, you will be promoted and presented before great people. God's plan will be small consistent steps that lead to bigger blessings.

Often, when God has given us an assignment or vision, we think of the fastest way to accomplish it. However, when it comes to the things of God, there's always a process involved. We can see the evidence in nature. When an apple seed is planted in the ground, it takes two to five years until the tree bears any fruit. After conceiving a baby, there's a nine-month process that every mother has to endure in order to give birth to that child. Why do we expect our prayers to be answered immediately, and why do we expect God to trust us with stewardship over life responsibilities we didn't work for?

Instant gratification is a common expectation that most people have, but being consistently diligent in the pursuit of a goal is as rare as a ten-carat diamond. "The plans of the diligent leads surely to advantage." (Proverbs 21:5)

A Word from the Lord

In this season, I have you hidden. When I unveil you, no one will know or understand where you came from. People will be amazed by your character, humility and wisdom. You will be blessed abundantly and you will continue to walk in grace, love and humility. Some will be jealous of you, but it will not impact you. You will continue to bless them and pray for them. Understand this: you can't do everything, and you can't do just anything. I have a specific calling for your life.

Your Process Of Peace

Take this time to clear your mind of everything you think you need and focus only on God. Breathe in and breathe out as you quiet your soul. Then think about the goodness of God and mediate in thanksgiving on who God is. He is a just God who properly blesses His children when we're faithful. Make a commitment to be diligent in the fulfillment of the calling assigned to your life.

Meditate on and affirm the following words

"Lord, I commit to be diligent and work as unto You in everything I do."

Scripture

"Wealth from get-rich-quick schemes quickly disappears; wealth from hard work grows over time." (Proverbs 13:11)

Life Journaling

Make a list of the most important dreams, desires or projects in your life.

____

____

____

____

____

Prioritize your list. Start with your most important dream.

____

____

____

____

____

Have you ever been involved in a get-rich-quick scheme?

____

____

____

____

____

How can you avoid seeking instant gratification?

Instead of creating a fast-results strategy for accomplishing your goals, write out a long-term plan that includes small, diligent tasks that lead to great results.

Elder David A. Bednar said, "Ordinary people who faithfully, diligently and consistently do simple things that are right before God will bring forth extraordinary results." What do you think he meant, and how can you follow his advice?

LIFE MESSAGE 2

THE PAINFUL PROGRESSION

"The moment you're ready to quit is usually the moment right before a miracle happens. Don't give up."

–Unknown

Progress is a good thing. It is movement and development towards your destination. When you're progressing, you're gradually advancing in the direction of accomplishing your goal. It's a wonderful thing, but it can also be painful.

Our spirits hunger and thirst to be filled. We desire the fullness of God. However, during the progression season, you'll experience small milestones and see gradual evidence of the coming breakthrough. In this season, you are not where you were in the past. You are in a much better place.

The small improvements and gradual increases are inspiring, but they can also be discouraging. It's like going to the best restaurant in the world and being served by a top award-winning chef. You are extremely hungry because you haven't eaten in hours, but the smell of all the tasty food excites you. You can see all the different people at their tables smiling and eating their gourmet meals, and everything looks amazingly good. You look over the menu filled with delicious-looking meals, and it's hard to choose, because you want it all. You start ordering appetizers, drinks, entrées and desserts, and your mouth is watering because you can taste and feel the food in your mouth before it comes. However, when your waitress brings out your meal, you are only given a teaspoon's taste of everything. You eat it and feel better than you felt before you came to the restaurant, but you want more. The small tastes are like a tease; it's progress but not fulfillment. It's a painful progression that motivates you to acknowledge the improvement in your situation but makes you yearn for more each time. As the waitress comes around again and again, you are only gradually satisfied.

If this was your experience at a restaurant, you would be upset, right? I would probably demand more food right away or a refund. Most of us would be frustrated and angry. In reality, this is how it feels when you're progressing towards your breakthrough. The pain of progressive experience is the reason many give up before ever reaching their breakthrough. But when you are in progress, that is exactly where God wants you.

"Do not despise these small beginnings, for the Lord rejoices to see the work begin." (Zechariah 4:10)

Our human nature despises small beginnings; but God loves them. He rejoices in seeing our progress begin. In the struggle of our small beginnings, God can build your character, patience and endurance.

"We can rejoice, when we run into trials, for we know that they help us develop endurance, and endurance develops strength of character and character strengthens our hope." (Romans 5:4)

It's necessary that you go through the process of progress in order to receive the blessings of your breakthrough. Your breakthrough is always on the other side of your greatest test. This is why everyone won't experience their breakthrough. Everyone isn't always willing to do what it takes to pass their greatest test.

The key is to get your mind off the gradual progress. Be thankful and appreciate your small improvements, but do not focus on them. Your focus must stay on consistently and diligently trusting that as you work on the plan, you will reap results. It may take months, years or even decades to complete; but God's grace is sufficient, and regardless of what you are working towards, He will strengthen you to do all things. Remember Philippians 4:13: "I can do all things through Christ who strengthens me."

This is why it's important that God strengthen your character, patience and endurance. If you're not properly prepared for your breakthrough, your breakthrough might break you.

In the book *Can You Stand To Be Blessed,* Bishop T.D. Jakes describes how he prayed that God would move mightily in his ministry. The Lord answered him by saying, "you are concerned about building a ministry, but I'm concerned about building a man." Then God said, "woe unto the man whose ministry becomes bigger than he is!"

God will never give you more than you can handle. He allows you to grow gradually because he loves you and He would never want His blessings to overwhelm and harm you. When you're not well prepared, too much of anything can become harmful. But when God sees you being faithful and accepting the gradual increases He grants you, He will trust you with more.

"If you are faithful in little things, you will be faithful in much. But if you are dishonest in little things, you will be dishonest with greater." (Luke 16:10) This verse describes how you will be tested, stretched and pushed beyond your current limits to see if you can handle the amount of blessings that are in store for you. Don't be discouraged, and don't allow your painful progression to intimidate you. Keep trusting God and diligently do the work you are called to do.

"Whatever you do, work at it with all your heart, as working for the Lord rather than people. Remember that the Lord will give you an inheritance as your reward, and that the Master you are serving is Christ." (Colossians 3:23-24)

Your Process Of Peace

Take this time to clear your mind and focus only on God. Breathe in and breathe out as you quiet your soul. Then think about the goodness of God, and mediate in thanksgiving on who God is. He will never give you more than you can bear. He is a good God who gradually increases your gifts as you progress towards your breakthrough.

Meditate on and affirm the following words

"All things are working together for my good. My breakthrough is in progress."

Scripture

"Let us not become weary in well doing, for in due season we shall reap, if we faint not." (Galatians 6:9)

Life Journaling

How have you dealt with painful progression?

____

____

____

____

____

What have been the most difficult moments in gradually moving towards your breakthrough?

____

____

____

____

____

What specific things you know you need to do in order to pass this trial?

____

____

____

____

____

What can you do to take your mind off your painful progression?

Bishop T.D. Jakes wrote that he prayed that God would move mightily in his ministry. The Lord answered him saying, “you are concerned about building a ministry, but I’m concerned about building a man.” Then God said, “woe unto the man whose ministry becomes bigger than he is!” How can you apply this wisdom in your life?

LIFE MESSAGE 3

THE DANGEROUS PURSUIT OF HAPPINESS

"Blessed is the one who does not walk in step with the wicked or stand in the way that sinners take or sit in the way the sinners take or sit in the company of mockers of God, but whose delight is in the law of the Lord, and who meditates on it day and night. That person is like a tree planted by the streams of water, which yields its fruit in season and whose leaf does not wither—whatever they do prospers."

–Psalms 1:1-3

You may be surprised to read the title of this life message and see that the pursuit of happiness can be dangerous. You may be thinking, what's wrong with pursuing happiness? Shouldn't we embrace being happy? Isn't life about being happy? Even the American Declaration of Independence declares that all have the right to, "Life, Liberty and the pursuit of Happiness." But let's consider what our pursuit of happiness could lead to.

A woman who's unhappy with her body image and career may believe pursuing happiness means taking out a second mortgage to hire a plastic surgeon to fix her body and invest in a new business after quitting her job. In her mind, taking out a mortgage on her house would give her the money she needs for the surgery and business. The business would help her free herself from work stress, and the surgery would make her body more attractive and appealing. She believes this will allow her to gain more love, success and happiness.

A man who's unhappy with his marriage and family may believe pursuing happiness means having an affair with another woman, taking a break from his kids and traveling the world, living his childhood dream of being an athlete. In his mind, these choices would make him feel happy and fulfilled and help him gain the respect, passion and attention that he lacks at home as he explores new adventures in life.

Have you ever heard the saying, "As long as you're happy, I'm happy?" People normally say this when they are trying to avoid judging someone or giving bad advice. It reflects a belief that happiness is the best way to judge if something is right or wrong and that if something makes you happy, then it's good. However, if we followed that logic in every area of life, we would have some problems. God never intended that we seek happiness. Instead, He tells us to "seek first the kingdom of God above all else, and live righteously and He will give you everything you need." (Matthew 6:33)

When you seek God above all else, you will never lack anything. The woman who was unhappy with her body image and career is now bankrupt from a failing business, and although the plastic surgeon gave her a new body, she gained weight from financial stress and overeating. She's in a much worse position now because she's unemployed, overweight and homeless after being unable to pay back her double mortgage. The man who had an affair and left his family to pursue his childhood dream of being an athlete is now divorced, lonely and disabled from a sports injury. His medical bills have taken much of his money, he has lost custody of his children, and his mistress left him when his money decreased. Both were pursing happiness, and in this pursuit, they both were left unhappy.

When it comes to happiness, the answer is never more money, success, fame or romantic love. Those things may seem to bring happiness, but in reality, all they give is a temporary feeling of pleasure with a lasting emptiness and addictive longing to gain more. Pursing happiness will never lead to your breakthrough, but the devastation that comes from pursuing happiness will lead to disappointment. As we walk the path leading to our undeniable breakthrough, it's important for us to be open to a new habit-based mindset that will create the results you desire in life.

Your Process Of Peace

Take this time to clear your mind of everything you think you need and focus only on God. Breathe in and breathe out as you quiet your soul. Then think about the goodness of God and meditate in thanksgiving on the many blessings He's allowed you to experience in life. He blessed you with life, health and intellect. There may be things you desire, but you have all you need.

Meditate on and affirm the following words

"I have everything I need. I lack nothing. I have everything I need in every moment, and even when I'm waiting, I have everything I need in this moment."

Scripture

"The Lord is my shepherd, I lack nothing." –Psalms 23:1

Life Journaling

In what area in your life do you desire an undeniable breakthrough and why?

____

____

____

____

____

How have you pursued happiness in the past?

____

____

____

____

____

How has pursing happiness left you disappointed?

____

____

____

____

____

What are your thoughts about pursing God?

____

____

____

____

____

Have you ever felt like God has forgotten about you? When?

____

____

____

____

____

Read Deuteronomy 31:6 and write out your thoughts.

____

____

____

____

____

Write out your thoughts about Psalms 23:1, which says, “I lack nothing.”

____

____

____

____

____

____

____

Mother Teresa said, “God has not called me to be SUCCESSFUL. He called me to be FAITHFUL.” What do you think she meant, and how can you be faithful to God?

____

____

____

____

____

____

____

____

____

____

LIFE MESSAGE 4

MAKING MY VISION MY REALITY

"Casting down imaginations and every high thing that exalts itself against the knowledge of God, and bringing into captivity every thought to the obedience of Christ."

–2 Corinthians 10:5

Many years ago, God gave me a vision. When I first received the vision, it was almost unbelievable to me. It seemed too big to manifest. After a while, I began to believe I could accomplish the vision. I created a plan, invested in the vision and went to work to make the vision become my reality. Instead of me seeking God for direction and answers, I sought the vision. My life was filled with the busyness of making my dream come true. It was very difficult for me to live in the present moment because I kept seeing the big vision. I couldn't get it off my mind, I wanted it so badly. I thought God wanted me to want it because He gave it to me and made it a desire of my heart.

My relationships suffered during this season of my life, and I made bad financial decisions as well. I dealt with health issues from the stress and anxiety of making that vision my reality, only to fail over and over again. When I was around loved ones, I was never fully present in the moment. My mind was always somewhere in the future, trying to complete a task. My to-do list never ended. I was too fearful to rest, and I didn't believe I had enough time to pray, fast or seek God. I wanted to be successful, and I wanted to make my vision my reality. I didn't realize I was living a dangerous fantasy that was blocking my breakthrough.

One morning, I made myself ignore my to-do-list and seek God in prayer, meditation and journaling. During this time in my life, I had committed myself to a major project and had already lost money, sleep and peace of mind, but I was determined to complete the final event of this project. I had told hundreds of people about it. I had promoted it and gotten several partners, staff and volunteers committed. I was tired, stress and fearful because I had risked so much. During this particular morning prayer, God asked me did I surrender my life completely to Him. Of course I said, "Yes, God, I give you my all I will lay everything down unto You." Then I heard God say, "Would you cancel the final event of this project?"

In that moment, I realized I had been pushing so hard to quickly manifest my vision, but in that moment I began to embrace the current moment. I could see my truth and where I was in reality. I wrote this in my journal, "I see a vision, but it seems like it will take forever when I look at where I am now." When I focused on my vision, I lived a fantasy that told me I was almost there, but when I analyzed my truth and embraced my current reality, I could see how far I really was from making my vision my reality.

Some people never want to receive the truth because they don't want to destroy their illusions. But you must be willing to face the reality of your current moment and follow God, allowing only Him to manifest His vision and will for your life.

When you're in your season of breakdown, it may seem as if everything around you is falling apart. You may encounter hardship in your relationships, finances and health. During this season, it's encouraging to envision blessings in every area of your life. It's important that you remain positive and hopeful while seeking the Lord, but sometimes, hopeful visions become dangerous fantasies. Your fantasies, dreams and imagination can become blessing blockers that stand in the way of your breakthrough.

You may ask, "how could my vision and dreams become harmful to me? Shouldn't we visualize positive things that encourage us during our darkest moments? Shouldn't we fill our minds with hope?"

Yes, but only to a certain extent. The Bible specifies, "Finally, brethren, whatsoever things are true, whatsoever things are honest, whatsoever things are just, whatsoever things are pure, whatsoever things are lovely, whatsoever things are of good report; if there be any virtue, and if there be any praise, think on these things." (Philippians 4:8)

Moreover, as you fill your mind with what is true, honest, just, pure, lovely and of good report, always remember to embrace it *now*. Here's the issue: its tempting to use "positive thinking" as a way of escape, and in doing so, people begin to live a fantasy without ever facing reality. Their visions become their objects of worship and glorification rather than God. Your vision can block your breakthrough when you seek the vision above God. When you're this focused on your vision, you will have a difficult time knowing the will of God and fulfilling His true vision and purpose for your life.

There's a difference between good and God. We should seek not a good idea but a God idea. We should pursue a God vision, not a good vision. You should never stop seeking God consistently as you work to achieve the vision He has given you. "The one who works his land will have plenty of food, but whoever chases fantasies lack sense." (Proverbs 12:11)

When you experience hardship, its important to know its okay. It's okay to be sad, hurt, angry and mad. That's part of your life; just don't live there forever. Experience it and move forward to healing. When you live in the present moment and embrace your reality, you can heal from pain, analyze and create a realistic strategy to enhance every area of your life.

Your Process Of Peace

Take this time to clear your mind of everything you think you need and focus only on God. Breathe in and breathe out as you quiet your soul. Then think about the goodness of God and meditate in thanksgiving on who God is. He is the God of visions, dreams and imaginations. Exalt Him above all and ask Him to lead and guide you. Surrender all your hopes, dreams, desires and wants to Him.

Meditate on and affirm the following words

"Lord I surrender all my plans, visions, and desires to You. Have your way in my life."

Scripture

"Casting down imaginations and every high thing that exalts itself against the knowledge of God, and bringing into captivity every thought to the obedience of Christ." (2 Corinthians 10:5)

Life Journaling

What fantasy, dreams and imaginations could become blessing blockers in your life?

____

____

____

____

____

Have you ever sought after a vision above God?

____

____

____

____

____

How have you struggled with living in the present moment?

____

____

____

____

____

Have you ever found yourself too focused on making your dreams come true instead of seeking the true purpose and will of God?

Which visions in your life are suffering right now for a breakthrough?

Have you given those visions to God, or have you tried to create them yourself?

Helen Keller said, “If the blind put their hands in God’s, they find their way more surely than those who see but have no faith or purpose.” What do you think she meant, and how can you follow her advice?

LIFE MESSAGE 5

FINDING PURPOSE IN THE PAIN

"The Lord is near to the brokenhearted and saves the crushed in spirit."
–Psalms 34:18

I cringed as I walked on that bus. My heart was racing fast, the palm of my hands were sweating, and I could feel drops of fear consistently traveling through my stomach. I couldn't catch my breath, and my fear grew intensely. Shortly after I sat in my seat, the bus began moving. I could hear her voice growing through the chaotic noise. "Where is Rainie?" she yelled. "Oh, I see her ugly moon face." I knew she was about to get started.

I had suffered in silence for months as the entire bus of middle school kids laughed at her words. The painful words were gradually destroying my fragile self-worth. I wanted to vanish, disappear and no longer suffer in silence. I had become depressed and tormented in my spirit from the traumatic, toxic abuse. The verbal abuse had become so bad that I started to despise how I looked, I wanted to change things about my face, and I hated looking in the mirror. I started to hate my life. It felt like I lived in a dark world. I was twelve years old and in the seventh grade. I didn't like confrontation, and I wanted to be accepted by others. Willow had spend almost the entire school year bullying me and whoever else she felt she could take advantage of.

This was one of the darkest seasons of my life. I felt a spirit of torment weighing heavily on me, and I had no rest. I wanted to become free, but I didn't know how.

During this time in my life, my family went to church on Sundays, but I didn't feel close to God. I had many questions about God, and I wanted evidence and proof of God, not just religion and ritual. I wanted to know God personally. One Wednesday night, my mom took me to a youth ministry meeting. That night, the minister spoke of receiving the Holy Spirit and how the power of the Holy Spirit living in you will change your life. She said, "the Holy Spirit will come and dwell in you, and if you ask, the Holy Spirit can heal and deliver you from anything you're dealing with." She reminded us of John 16:13: "But when He, the Spirit of truth, comes, He will guide you into all the truth; for He will not speak on His own initiative, but whatever He hears, He will speak; and He will disclose to you what is to come."

I wanted a spiritual encounter with God, and when the minister asked if anyone needed prayer, I was the only one who stood up. I wasn't afraid of what others would think of me. I was desperate for help, and I wanted the darkness and depression to end. I went to a back room for prayer, and the minister led me to pray, "I confess with my mouth that Jesus is Lord and believe in my heart that God raised Him from dead. I am now saved." (Romans 10:9)

I begin thanking God, and all of a sudden I felt this powerful, peaceful presence that I had never felt before. Immediately, a new spiritual language began to flow from my mouth. I was no longer in control, but the spirit of God was flowing through me. I was amazed as an unknown language boldly gave forth from my mouth. Tears fell from my eyes as I gratefully acknowledged God's miraculous truth. I left that meeting saying to myself, "Wow, God is real." The Father, Son and Holy Spirit were no longer just the God my mom served. He became my God.

The very next morning, before I got on the school bus to face Willow the bully, I prayed in the Holy Spirit. God's presence began to flow as I prayed, although I didn't understand what was going on. I believed God was working everything out in the spiritual realm and eventually His grace would manifest in the physical realm. Then the torment, depression and bullying stopped completely. Willow never said another word to me or about me. At first I thought it was strange to see her look at me without saying a word. I later realized that God had closed her mouth completely concerning me.

Over twenty years have passed since then, and until recently, I have always wondered what happened to Willow. In my mind, I have always imagined her being in a terrible place in her life. She was obese as a child, so in my mind, I have always expected her to be overweight and miserable as an adult. She was so evil and cruel that I could never imagine her living a happy life. I had been set free from her abuse, and I saw the situation as a stepping stone that helped me understand abuse, depression and despair, but secretly, I hoped she suffered.

However, more recently, I realized I had forgiven her and actually saw my experience with her as a blessing because her abuse led me to start my nonprofit, Sisters of Hope. So many positive things came from that experience that I thought about thanking her, and I looked for her on Facebook. It was astonishing to witness my own reaction after seeing pictures of her as an adult on Facebook. She was unrecognizable. She had lost weight. She was into health and fitness, and she also seemed to be a happy person. The better, newer part of me was happy for her, but I couldn't ignore my simultaneous uncomfortable feeling of disappointment. I was disappointed because in the fantasy in my mind, Willow was strung out on drugs, in prison and overweight. That had been my own selfish way of gaining revenge in the physical world. I had imagined that I would see evidence of torment, and I had wanted payback. I needed to remind myself that God had already restored me, healed me and vindicated the situation. God has used me to help people all over the world because of the pain of my past.

If someone has hurt you and made your life more challenging, you may not get the revenge you desire to see, but you must understand that when someone is abusive to you, it's not about you. You are not the issue. It's all about what's going on inside that person that leads them to plant seeds of toxic abuse. You can use that season of your life to grow by gaining strength and supernatural power in the Lord, or you can allow it to darken your heart. My season gave me strength in the end, but I needed to be broken in order to experience that breakthrough.

That abusive experience was the beginning of many life breakthroughs for me. The biggest was that I began to develop a relationship with God. I talked to Him about my relationships and the blessings I desired in my life, and to my amazement, He responded. I started writing my prayers to God, and as He spoke back and, I wrote what I believed He was saying. In the beginning, I would mistake God's voice with my own. However, after years of practice, I grew to hear the difference, and I matured spiritually in the process. I was training myself spiritually. "Instead, train yourself to be godly. Physical training is good, but training for godliness is much better, promising benefits in this life and in the life to come." (1 Timothy 4:7-8)

There were times when I prayed selfishly for the wrong things and God allowed me to have them just to teach me a lesson. Whenever I sinned and turned away from God, He patiently corrected me and gave me the courage to overcome my mistakes. I even experienced seasons when I took time off from praying and fasting, but God was always there when I came back. I've learned that the more I draw near to God, the more He draws near to me. (James 4:8)

Your Process Of Peace

Take this time to clear your mind and focus only on God. Breathe in and breathe out as you quiet your soul. Then think about the goodness of God and meditate in thanksgiving on who God is. Understand that there's purpose in your pain. God wants to heal and deliver you from it all. Allow Him to move in your life. Draw near to Jesus.

Meditate on and affirm the following words

"The more difficult something is, the more God is going to multiply my blessings. I'm not going to come out the same. I'm going to come out better than I was before."

Scripture

"You meant it for evil, but God meant it for good." (Genesis 50:20)

Life Journaling

Have you ever doubted God?

____

____

____

____

____

____

What was the most painful season you've experienced in your life?

____

____

____

____

____

____

____

____

____

____

Right before your breakthrough, it always gets the hardest. You may want to give up and quit. Every single thing in the natural world may feel like it's breaking down. Instead of giving up, how can you allow God to lead you to your breakthrough?

LIFE MESSAGE 6

BREAKING DOWN BEFORE BREAKING THROUGH

"The sacrifice you desire is a broken spirit. You will not reject a broken and repentant heart, O God."

–Psalms 51:17

We live in a society that labels broken, hurt people as weak and miserable. Often, when we go through tough seasons, instead of allowing ourselves to mourn, we try to suck it up. We bury our pain and hurt in an effort to appear strong. Instead of crying and freely letting out our painful emotions, we hide them with a smile. We become professional actors and actresses wearing daily masks that hide our true identity. As women, we mask our pain with makeup, new hairstyles and fashionable attire. In our minds, we treat what we look like on the outside as more important than how we feel on the inside. We believe grief is only for funerals.

When you go through a separation, divorce, breakup or any other loss, it's okay to grieve. Grief is essential to your health. If you never get sad about anything, something is wrong. You're either out of touch with reality, out of touch with your emotions, or you don't love. Grief is a healthy emotion. "God blesses those who mourn, for they will be comforted." (Matthew 5:4)

When you allow yourself to mourn your loss, God will bless and comfort you. Grief is the gift God gives us to get through the transitions of life. "There is no growth in your life without change; there is no change without loss; there is no loss without pain and there is no pain without grief." (Rick Warren)

You must give yourself permission to break down before you can experience your breakthrough. Don't do like some people who deal with pain by blocking it out of their minds. That's a sign of living in denial. If you don't let it out, you will act it out.

As a little girl, I didn't know how to respond to pain. I saw violence and verbal and physical abuse. I experienced the pain of my father being abusive towards my mother, and as a four-year-old I was scared. He was in and out of prison, and I didn't understand that his behavior was not normal. I didn't know how to grieve. I became very shy and quiet. I didn't talk much. I didn't cry either, because I didn't understand that what I felt was pain. I didn't know how to mourn in a healthy way.

When you don't grieve the losses in your life, you will get stuck at the stage at which you suffered those losses. Swallowing negative emotions will make you sick mentally and physically. I'm sure you've heard the saying, "It's not what you eat. It's what's eating you." I grew up in a home where we didn't address issues. We didn't talk about our feelings. We always pretended as if everything was good. I can't recall ever hearing my parents apologize for anything. There was always a feeling that, no matter what, they were right because they were my parents. It took years for me to realize they were not always right. Even if you're a parent, it's okay to express your feelings when you're troubled. It's important for parents to lead their children in humility and love and always be willing to apologize when they are wrong. Children respect parents more when they do.

As you allow yourself to be broken, its important to not become silent and hold everything inside. Talk to a trusted friend or family member. "For when I kept silent, my bone wasted away through my groaning all day long." (Psalm 32:3) "I was mute and silent; I held my peace to no avail, and my distress grew worse." (Psalm 39:2)

Remember that God blesses those who mourn, so don't be ashamed or afraid to show your pain. The Bible says when we mourn, God draws us close to Himself. (Psalms 34:18) Give yourself time to mourn. Some of the losses in your life may be extremely detrimental, and sometimes people will not understand. You may never get over it, but you can get through it. You can't go around, under or above the pain, but God will help you go through it. Don't allow fear to hold you back from facing the pain. When you get through it, you will come out stronger. "Sometimes it takes a painful experience to make us change our ways." (Proverbs 20:30)

Your Process Of Peace

Take this time to clear your mind and focus only on God. Breathe in and breathe out as you quiet your soul. Then think about the goodness of God and meditate in thanksgiving on who God is. As you draw closer to God, He will give you the strength to go through your pain by showing you His purpose. As you understand that there's purpose in the pain, as there is in the pain of laboring to have a baby, you will gain strength. When you see no purpose, it's easy to give up.

Meditate and affirm the following words

"My God is walking me through my breakdown before He releases my breakthrough."

Scripture

"For everything there is a season, and a time for every matter under the heaven; a time to weep, and a time to laugh; a time to mourn, and a time to dance." (Ecclesiastes 3:1, 4)

Life Journaling

How do you usually hide your pain?

____

____

____

____

____

____

What are the losses in your life that you've never grieved?

____

____

____

____

____

____

____

____

____

____

____

____

What pain did you experience as a child?

____

____

____

____

____

____

____

____

____

How do you deal with pain now?

____

____

____

____

____

____

____

____

____

____

Rick Warren said "There is no growth in your life without change, there is no change without loss, there is no loss without pain, and there is no pain without grief." How can you apply this wisdom in your life?

LIFE MESSAGE 7

HEARING GOD'S VOICE & RECEIVING YOUR BREAKTHROUGH

"My sheep listen to my voice; I know them, and they follow me."
–John 10:27

There have been times in my life when I stopped asking God what He wanted for my life and started asking myself what *I* wanted for my life. As I mentioned in chapter 4, my ego inspired me to believe that I could create the life I wanted. In that season, I maintained my faith in God, but I began to believe more in myself. That selfish mentality led me to pursue people, money and success above God. I started believing that money could buy my happiness and a better life for my family. That belief led me to stop chasing God and start chasing worldly success.

I had to learn the hard way that God must always come first. He must lead and guide our paths, not our self-esteem or worldly success. Although there's nothing wrong with having confidence and financial wealth, it can't have you. The bible says that "No one can serve two masters. For you will hate one and love the other; you will be devoted to one and despise the other. You cannot serve both God and money." (Matthew 6:24)

You may be thinking that you could never serve God over money. But ask yourself, have you ever taken a job because the pay was good without getting confirmation from God? Have you ever started a business without hearing from God first? Have you ever invested in something without praying first? Did the amount of money involved lead you to that choice, or did God lead you? "If you chase money, money will always outrun you. If you forget about money and focus on serving God, money will chase you." (Miles Monroe)

"Whoever loves money never has enough, whoever loves wealth is never satisfied with their income. This too is meaningless." –Ecclesiastes 5:10

During this season of chasing money and success, I began to think I needed professional mentors and associations to help me get to higher levels in my life. I started trusting in degrees, certifications and expertise to give me what I was seeking. It sounds so foolish as I write this, but it's true. I didn't verbally say it out loud, but I thought it. Don't get me wrong. I never stopped worshipping and loving God. I just began to become so consumed with gaining accomplishments and success that God no longer had top priority in my life.

I became too busy to pray. I had lots of business meetings and tasks to complete on my to-do list. There was no time for God. I was always working, always stressed and always tired. My weight was out of control, I wasn't getting enough sleep, and there was no rest for my soul. The more I chased the cares of this world (success, wealth, people-approval, etc.), the more I felt unfulfilled and discontented. I was always comparing my life to someone else's. I was never satisfied.

When I did pray, I often felt like something was blocking my prayers from being effective. I found myself reading various self-help books that gave new-age spirituality advice. My spirit hungered and thirsted for the Lord, but in my mind, I thought reading the Bible wouldn't help because I already knew the Bible. My pride and ego led me to believe I already knew everything about God and the Bible and it was time that I explored something new. As I reflect back on those thoughts, I realize how wrong I was. All those beliefs were lies planted in my mind to keep me from rekindling my relationship with God. After being exhausted from working extremely hard and getting nowhere, carrying my baggage of anxiety and stress, God told me that I could let it all go and come to Him and He would give me rest for my soul.

"Then Jesus said, "Come to me, all of you who are weary and carry heavy burdens, and I will give you rest." (Matthew 11:28)

The truth is, God never called me to chase success or compare myself to others. He didn't call any of us to strive to be better than anyone else. I'm not here to be the greatest and most successful; that's the mindset of the systems of this world. God called us to fulfill the purpose and calling He has given us, and we are to do it in the grace, peace and rest of God. "Jesus said, my yoke is easy and my burden is light." (Matthew 11:30)

Whenever you compare yourself with others because you believe you lack something they possess or feel discontent with your life, that's a sign that your spirit is hungry and thirsty for God. That's a sign that you're trying to fill an empty void that nothing or nobody can fill but God. When you fill up with God, you lack nothing! "But those who trust in the LORD will lack no good thing."- Psalm 34:10

My breakthrough test was for me to understand that it's not all about me and that I can't do anything apart from God. I must seek God daily through worship, prayer and journaling. I no longer believe I can accomplish anything without Jesus. Without His guidance and confirmation, I'm lost. I will not start my day without seeking God. I won't start a project without His guidance. I must hear from God before writing a book; I need His direction in every chapter and word.

I encourage you to seek the Lord before starting a career, relationship, business and any other endeavor in your life. My heart goes out to everyone who starts a relationship without seeking God first. God was my divine matchmaker in my marriage. He brought my husband into my life after I surrendered that area of my life to Him. I share more about this story in my book, *When God Sent My Husband*.

It's important that we become rooted and grounded in our faith in Christ Jesus. God has specific things He wants to do in specific seasons of your life. It's up to you to jump on board and go where God is leading you. He will never force it. When we become distracted and consumed with the cares of this world, we miss God. God's voice is very quiet in a loud world, and the only way we can hear Him is by turning down the noise around us and seeking Him. Praying and Fasting always bring us closer to God and make His voice louder in our lives.

You may be asking, "how can I hear God's voice, and how do I know it's not my own voice?" There is a method and process to opening your spiritual ears to hear the voice of God. Apply these five wisdoms to learn how to hear from God.

1. First, you need to start with worship. Worship is the doorway to receive revelations from God. When you worship God first, you are acknowledging your love, trust and dependency on the Lord.
2. As you worship and put your mind and focus on God, He will often give you a word. Sometimes its only one word. The Bible speaks of the word of the Lord being quickened and made to come alive by the Holy Spirit. As you allow the Holy Spirit to flow into you, the word of God will become alive for you and your situation.
3. It's important that you have faith in the word that God declares in your life. God will give to you according to your portion of faith, and more faith comes when you pay attention to the word of God every day. The more you hear God's word through His scriptures and teachings, the more your faith will increase.

4. You may have questions or seek direction on what to do about a particular situation. God says ask, seek and knock (Matthew 7:7-11). Don't be afraid to begin a conversation with God.
5. Learn the voice of God. God will speak to your spirit, and His voice sounds similar to your own. That's because God speaks through your personality. The difference between your voice and God's is that His words add life to your spirit. His words will quench an inner thirst. Wisdom, clarity and divine direction come from His spirit.

As you experience your breakthrough, you must understand the spiritual discipline required to draw you closer to God. One of the most powerful forms of spiritual discipline is fasting. Fasting is refraining from food for a spiritual purpose. Fasting will bring you into a deeper, more intimate and more powerful relationship with God. In Jentezen Franklin's book *Fasting*, he says, "When you eliminate food from your diet for a number of days, your spirit becomes uncluttered by the things of this world and amazingly sensitive to the things of God." When you fast, you will become more sensitive to the voice of God, hearing Him clearly. Keep this in mind: don't come to God with your needs, but come to God to learn of your needs. Instead of telling God what you want, ask God what He desires for you to have.

Your Breakthrough

Pain will motivate you to change. Sometimes you have to hit bottom in order to remember to look to God. Your breakthrough is always on the other side of your battle. Many people miss their breakthrough because they're not willing to get through the battle. It will require discipline and diligence. It may take longer than you expected. The battle may take longer because God wants to see if you're capable of handling the blessing. You are being stretched and tested beyond your limitations. Don't give up; you can weather the storm. The best is yet to come, and when it becomes the worst you have experienced, you are about to receive your breakthrough.

A Word from the Lord

I want to bless you. I want to use you to make a difference in the lives of others. Give Me your all. Grow gradually as I lead you. Don't become anxious and move ahead of Me. I must lead you first. You must receive My confirmation first. Give as I lead your heart.

Your Process Of Peace

Take this time to clear your mind and focus only on God. Breathe in and breathe out as you quiet your soul. Then think about the goodness of God and meditate in thanksgiving on who God is. Ask God to lead and guide your way. Give Him your desires in exchange for His purpose, and allow Him to release your breakthrough.

Meditate on and affirm the following words

"I will commit to faithfulness, consistency and contentment while being hungry for God, and in doing so, I will earn His blessings."

Scripture

"Father, if you are willing, please take this cup of suffering away from me. Yet I want your will to be done, not mine." (Luke 22:42)

Life Journaling

Have you ever sought your own will instead of God's will for your life?

In what way have you chased worldly success?

Miles Monroe said, “If you chase money, money will always outrun you. If you forget about money and focus on serving God, money will chase you.” How can you apply that advice to your life?

CONCLUSION

After reading this book and applying its strategies to your life, you will be ready for your undeniable breakthrough. When you experience this type of breakthrough, there is no question or doubt about the transformation coming in your life. It will be evident to everyone who comes into contact with you. The change will be obvious. When God moves in your life, He doesn't just reform. He renews. You become a new person. The Bible says, "Therefore, if anyone is in Christ he becomes a new person. The old life is gone; a new life has begun!" (2 Corinthians 5:17) Embrace the new life.

This is the reality of growth: when you are transitioning to a new season of life, there will be people, places and things that no longer fit your life. Don't fight the process of change; allow your life to flow in a new direction. Understand this: if they can't grow with you, then they can't go with you.

I want to connect with you. Send me your testimony at contact@rainiehoward.com or through through social media @RainieHoward to tell me how this book has blessed your life. Include the hashtags #RainieHoward and #UndeniableBreakthrough when you post photos and reviews of the book. You can also get free resources by connecting with me through my website www.RealLoveExist.com.

Are you addicted to a toxic love?

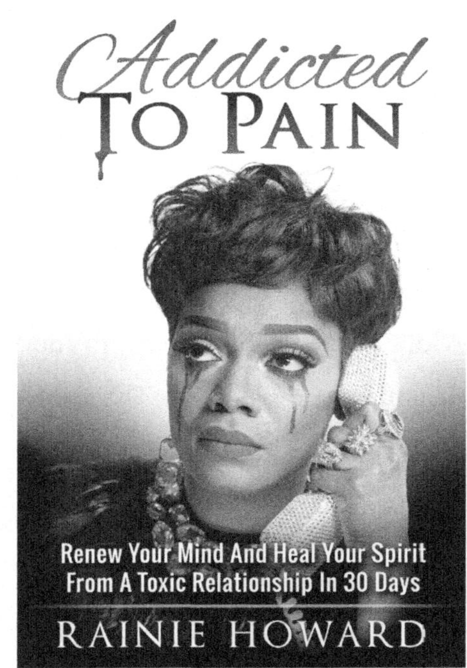

The obsession of a toxic relationship can have the same enticement as drugs or alcohol. The pattern echoes time and time again: a new significant other draws you into a new relationship that starts off loving and alluring only to develop into a hurtful or abusive cycle. A person who has a healthy understanding of "true love" does not tolerate this kind of pain. He or she will move on in search of a healthier bond. It's an unhealthy view of love that will rationalize toxic behavior and cling to a relationship long after it should have ended. Like any other addiction, those hooked on a toxic love have little or no control over excessive urges to text, call, manipulate or beg for love, attention and affection. They want help. They want to end the pain and recover, but it's just like trying to shake a drug habit.

In *Addicted to Pain,* author and relationship expert Rainie Howard reveals the truths every woman needs to heal from a toxic relationship and return to a life rich with purpose and fulfillment. This all-in-one spiritual guide provides daily insights on love addiction and a healing plan to help you recover from the overwhelming effects of a toxic relationship.

Have you been praying for a husband?

It's not easy being single, and when you have a vision to be married, it's challenging to patiently wait for the right one. It's important to understand that God has a divine purpose for your life and that He wants to gift you with the right man. *When God Sent My Husband* is a single women's guide to gaining wisdom on:

- How to guard your heart yet freely love
- Preparing and positioning yourself to receive love
- Building a solid foundation that captures and keeps love

In this book, Rainie Howard shares her personal story of seeking love, dating and embracing the divine experience of God bringing her husband into her life. This is a miraculous story of God being the ultimate matchmaker. The book will encourage you to take a spiritual approach to dating and preparing for marriage.

YOUR GIFT

As a thank-you for purchasing my book, I'm giving you free access to join "The Love Class" and the "Toxic Love Detox Challenge."

The Love Class is six weeks of videos, emails, love projects and dating and marriage advice. Go to http://bit.ly/LoveClass to join!

The Toxic Love Detox Challenge is a seven-day challenge that includes videos, inspirational healing messages and audio downloads. Go to http://bit.ly/toxiclovedetox to join. Learn the secrets to attracting real love and detoxifying your spirit from the hurt, pain and resentment that comes from a toxic relationship.

Don't forget to review this book on Amazon! You can use the following link: http://bit.ly/ReviewUBreakthrough

ABOUT THE AUTHOR

Rainie Howard is a wife, mother and mentor. She has authored several books including *Addicted To Pain* and *When God Sent My Husband.* She is a sought-after speaker and founder of Sisters of Hope, an organization that promotes women's empowerment. Rainie's mission is to share the love of Christ with people who are hurting all over the world. She and her husband, Patrick Howard, are the founders of "RealLoveExist," a movement that promotes real love stores and healthy marriages, encouraging others to never give up on love.

To learn more go to www.RealLoveExist.com

LIFE JOURNAL

LIFE JOURNAL

LIFE JOURNAL

LIFE JOURNAL

LIFE JOURNAL

LIFE JOURNAL

LIFE JOURNAL

LIFE JOURNAL

LIFE JOURNAL

LIFE JOURNAL

LIFE JOURNAL

LIFE JOURNAL

LIFE JOURNAL

LIFE JOURNAL

LIFE JOURNAL

LIFE JOURNAL

LIFE JOURNAL

LIFE JOURNAL

LIFE JOURNAL

LIFE JOURNAL

LIFE JOURNAL

LIFE JOURNAL

LIFE JOURNAL

LIFE JOURNAL

LIFE JOURNAL

LIFE JOURNAL

LIFE JOURNAL

LIFE JOURNAL

LIFE JOURNAL

LIFE JOURNAL

LIFE JOURNAL

LIFE JOURNAL

LIFE JOURNAL

LIFE JOURNAL

LIFE JOURNAL

LIFE JOURNAL

LIFE JOURNAL

LIFE JOURNAL

LIFE JOURNAL

LIFE JOURNAL

LIFE JOURNAL

LIFE JOURNAL

LIFE JOURNAL

LIFE JOURNAL

LIFE JOURNAL

LIFE JOURNAL

LIFE JOURNAL

LIFE JOURNAL

LIFE JOURNAL

LIFE JOURNAL

LIFE JOURNAL

Made in the USA
Middletown, DE
13 January 2023